I'm in a Mood Today

Poems about feelings

Collected by

John Foster

OXFORD
UNIVERSITY PRESS

Great Clarendon Street, Oxford OX2 6DP
Oxford University Press is a department of the University of Oxford.
It furthers the University's objective of excellence in research, scholarship,
and education by publishing worldwide in

Oxford New York

Athens Auckland Bangkok Bogotá Buenos Aires Calcutta
Cape Town Chennai Dar es Salaam Delhi Florence Hong Kong Istanbul
Karachi Kuala Lumpur Madrid Melbourne Mexico City Mumbai
Nairobi Paris São Paulo Singapore Taipei Tokyo Toronto Warsaw

with associated companies in Berlin Ibadan

Oxford is a registered trade mark of Oxford University Press
in the UK and in certain other countries

First published 2000

British Library Cataloguing in Publication Data available

ISBN 0-19-276229 X (hardback)
ISBN 0-19-276230 3 (paperback)

Printed in Hong Kong

Contents

JEERS AND TEARS

SKULKING IN SHADOWS

WHO CARES?

ON THE OUTSIDE, LOOKING IN

LOOKING TO THE FUTURE

Stepping in Sunlight

S-t-r-e-t-c-h-i-n-g

Waking up
in the morning
is lovely.
Especially when you s-t-r-e-t-c-h.
You open up
your legs and arms
and stretch.
It's just lovely.
The feeling just makes
you want to do it
over and over again.
But after a while
your stretch
runs out
and it's over.

Sharon Cheeks

The Sun in Me

The sun is in me,
pale morning flames
setting my still-sleeping
heart alight.

The wind is in me,
clear blue breath
leading my bare feet
into a new day.

The sea is in me,
deep green waves
whispering wild music
in my ears.

The river is in me,
dark brown waters
swirling its questions
around my head.

The moon is in me,
sad silver beams
painting my dreams
with shadows.

Moira Andrew

Acrostic

Debonaire,

Elegant,

Brilliant,

Jovial,

All describe me very well.

Not accurately, perhaps, but

In my dreams I am all these and more.

Debjani Chatterjee

First Leap

Because the hedge was there
he jumped it.

His mother saw
the scratches on his legs,
the snags on socks
so he jumped again
and this time
cleared it.

He felt the shock of the ground
as his feet struck home
bone thud on bone-hard earth.

But first, as he leapt,
he felt his limbs' weight drain out
felt, as birds do, the air as it turned
felt his blood blaze round
as his fist
hauled on the rope that he could see now
dangling clear as anything
from air to earth
for him!

Berlie Doherty

Mountain

Real joy
first bubbles up
before you reach the top:
the summit's there, ahead, just steps
away.

You stop,
stare, breathe deeply.
Joy, weightless, invades legs,
lungs, heart, and face; success is in
your grasp!

Judith Nicholls

Special Day

There was one special day I remember,
   when the sun set fire to the sky,
and I was at the blue-rimmed beach,
and I ran skidding down the steep green hill
   to the silver-glinting shore.
The white-topped waves swung skywards recklessly,
maybe trying to put out the fire in the sky.
I thrust myself at the ocean,
   snatching for action,
not wanting to waste one greedy moment,
not wanting to miss one searching wave.
It was a good day, that special day,
it had a good beginning,
   and no real ending;
there were no clocks out there
   where the waves wallowed on the sand;
no trannies screamed out the seconds
   and the minutes
   and the hours . . .
Eventually, I suppose, the day ended,
and the night must have swallowed up the fire,
and I must have plodded up the green hill sometime.
Days have passed since then,
   days without number,
days and nights; time;
   oceans of time.
Yet that one day, that special day,
   clings on to me forever,
with the sun setting fire to the sky
   and the sand on the shore glinting silver,
   and the white-topped waves reaching out for me . . .

David Bateson

Days

Days fly by on holidays,
they escape like birds
released from cages.
What a shame you can't buy
tokens of time, save them up
and lengthen the good days,
or maybe you could tear out time
from days that drag, then pay it back
on holidays, wild days,
days you wish would last forever.
You could wear these days with pride,
fasten them like poppies to your coat,
or keep them in a tin, like sweets,
a confection of days
to be held on the tongue
and tasted, now and then.

Brian Moses

I'm in a mood today

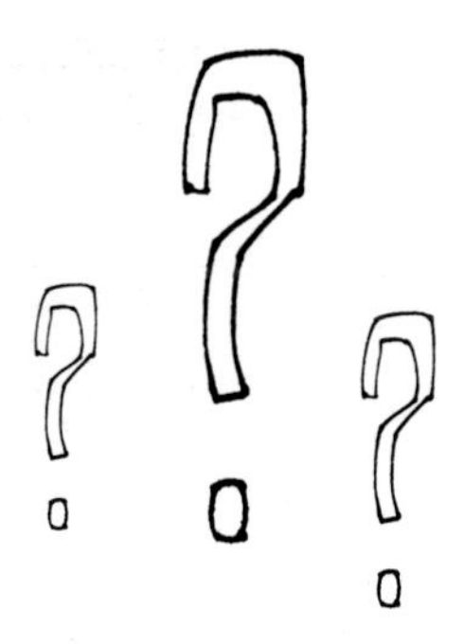

How Do I Feel?

How do I feel?
My face can't lie—

with furrowed brow
and narrowed eye

and zipped up teeth
that want to bite,

you'll know I'm looking
for a fight.

How do I feel?
My face can't lie—

it's like the sun
up in the sky,

with eyes like worms
bridged up to kiss,

I'm happy when
I look like this.

Gina Douthwaite

I'm in a Rotten Mood

I'm in a rotten mood today,
a really rotten mood today,
I'm feeling cross,
I'm feeling mean,
I'm jumpy as a jumping bean,
I have an awful attitude—
I'M IN A ROTTEN MOOD!

I'm in a rotten mood today,
a really rotten mood today,
I'm in a snit,
I'm in a stew,
there's nothing that I care to do
but sit all by myself and brood—
I'M IN A ROTTEN MOOD!

I'm in a rotten mood today,
a really rotten mood today,
you'd better stay away from me,
I'm just a lump of misery,
I'm feeling absolutely rude—
I'M IN A ROTTEN MOOD!

Jack Prelutsky

Huff

I am in a tremendous huff—
Really, really bad.
It isn't any ordinary huff—
It's one of the best I've had.

I plan to keep it up for a month
Or maybe for a year
And you needn't think you can make me smile
Or talk to you. No fear.

I can do without you and her and them—
Too late to make amends.
I'll think deep thoughts on my own for a while,
Then find some better friends.

And they'll be wise and kind and good
And bright enough to see
That they should behave with proper respect
Towards somebody like me.

I do like being in a huff—
Cold fury is so heady.
I've been like this for half an hour
And it's cheered me up already.

Perhaps I'll give them another chance,
Now I'm feeling stronger
But they'd better watch out—my next big huff
Could last much, much, much longer.

Wendy Cope

Boring

I'm dead bored,
  bored to the bone.
Nobody likes me,
  I'm all alone.
I'll just go crawl
  under a stone.

Hate my family,
  got no friends,
I'll sit here till
  the universe ends
Or I starve to death—
  it all depends.

Then I'll be dead,
  dead and rotten,
Less than a blot when
  it's been well blotten,
Less than a teddy bear
  that's been forgotten.

Then I'll go to Heaven which
  is more than can be said
For certain persons
  when they're dead.
They'll go you-know-
  where instead.

Then they'll be sorry,
  then they'll be glum,
Sitting on a stove till
  Kingdom Come.
Then they can all go
  kiss my . . .

Hmm, that's a sort of swearing;
  people shouldn't swear.
I won't go to Heaven but
  I don't care,
  I don't care,
  I don't care.
I'll sit here and swear
  so there.

Except that it's boring . . .

John Whitworth

Scowling

When I see you
scowling
I want to turn you
upside down
and see you
smile!

Roger McGough

Cheer Up

On days
when you're feeling
dreadfully
down
and your forehead
is furrowed
by a bad
tempered
frown

and you're sad
and you're
blue
and you wish
you weren't
you . . .

pull your funniest
face
give your ghastliest
grin
then say
goodbye
to the mood
you're in.

Ann Bonner

A Head Full of Feelings

A clear space
white light
floating, soaring—
I'm high as a kite.

A head full of clouds
a rolling jungle
grey and black rumbles—
I'm fed up.

Lemon bright fizz, soda pop tizz
burping and bursting
to get out—
I'm in a daft mood.

In the deep dark
stars exploding
Catherine wheels spinning—
I'm confused.

Pale blue peace
wide-awake sleep
not a peep—
I'm day-dreaming.

Red fire crackling
leaping, eating
the edges of my mind—
I'm angry
and the whole world
better watch out!

Patricia Leighton

I Hate Being Dyslexic

I can't spell
I urge the words out, but they won't come.
There's a buzzing feeling inside my head
Stopping the letters coming out.
It's like a bee flying around,
Tearing up the words that I've just learnt
Jumbling the letters about
Sometimes I'm so annoyed I nearly give up.
I can't do sums, the numbers get all muddled up.
Mumbling to myself, numbers
Over and over again.
But I can't work out what to do with them.
I'm not an ordinary person
It makes me upset
I try to bang my head, bang away
The buzzing feeling
But it doesn't work.

Abigail Wright

Why Me?

'Why me?'
He asked that question a lot.
'Why me?'
He watched the others.
They could do what they liked when they liked.
They could eat what they liked.
While he . . .
'But you can have a perfectly normal life with diabetes,'
they said.
But all he had to say to that was,
'Why me? Why me?'
And nobody had an answer to that.

Marian Swinger

Big Fears

Twenty-five feet above Sian's house
hangs a thick wire cable
that droops and sags between
two electricity pylons.
A notice says it carries 320,000 volts
from one metallic scarecrow to the next,
then on to the next and the next
right across the countryside to the city.
The cable sways above Sian's council house
making her radio crackle and sometimes
making her telly go on the blink.

If it's a very windy night
Sian gets frightened because
she thinks the cable might snap,
fall onto the roof and electrocute
everyone as they sleep.

This is Sian's big fear.

Outside Matthew's bedroom there is
a tall tree—taller than the house.
In summer it is heavy with huge leaves.
In winter it stands lonely as a morning moon.

On a windy night Matthew worries
that the tree might be blown down
and crash through his bedroom window.
It would certainly kill him . . . and his cat
if it was sleeping under the bed
where it usually goes.

This is Matthew's big fear.

Outside Sam's bedroom there's nothing
but a pleasant view; meadows, hedges, sheep
and some distant gentle hills.
There's nothing sinister, nothing frightening,
nothing to worry about.

But at night, in the dark, Sam thinks
the darting shapes on the ceiling
are really the shadows
of a ghost's great cold hands and
that the night noises made by the water pipes
are the screeches and groans of attic skeletons.

John Rice

Night Fears

Dark fears,
as the dawn breaks
and the night fades and dies,
dissolve with shadows into light
and hope.

Marian Swinger

Family Matters

The Baby of the Family

Up on Daddy's shoulders
He is riding high—
The baby of the family,
A pleased, pork pie.
I'm tired and my feet are sore—
It seems all wrong.
He's lucky to be little
But it won't last long.

The baby of the family,
He grabs my toys
And when I grab them back he makes
A big, loud noise.
I mustn't hit him, so I chant
This short, sweet song:
'You're lucky to be little
But it won't last long.'

Everybody looks at him
And thinks he's sweet,
Even when he bellows 'No!'
And stamps his feet.
He won't be so amusing
When he's tall and strong.
It's lovely being little
But it won't last long.

Wendy Cope

Sisterly Love

Take my brother . . .
Please.
He's driving me
Round the bend.
Take him
Before he comes
To a sticky end
At his sister's hand.

Though yesterday he did
The kindest thing and
I wouldn't have swapped him
For the world,
Today you should see
How he's behaving!!

I'll pay you 50p
If you'll take him away.

A pound?

Well, how much then?

Done.
I'll start saving.

Frances Nagle

Everybody

She's good at everything
And everybody says she is.

I'm good for nothing
And you keep on telling me.

I wish you'd sometimes say
I'm good at something.

It's not my fault I don't like
Anything she's good at.

Why do you keep on telling me
What everybody says?

Who is everybody anyway?
It's all your fault.

John Mole

Kelly Jane Alone

In faded jeans
and anorak
I walk along
the railway track.

Disused for more than
twenty years,
it calms my thunder-
storm of tears.

The rails are going
who knows where
and I'd go too
but I don't dare.

The voices raised
in disarray
are long ago
and far away.

Wild flowers wave
like tiny flags
and there's a thrush
that drags and drags

a worm from deep
inside the grass.
The clouds are calm
and small, and cross

the sky beyond
the pylon there . . .
and I'd go too
but I don't dare.

The argument
that drove me from
the living room
dies and is gone.

In faded jeans
and anorak
I walk along
the railway track.

Fred Sedgwick

The Secret

My brother had a secret
That had screwed him up inside.
He said that he could trust me
And he needed to confide.

Like a weird pass-the-parcel,
The secret's handed on.
Now my brother's feeling better,
While I'm the screwed-up one.

For I can't forget his secret.
It won't leave me alone
And it's heavy in my stomach,
Like I've swallowed a great stone.

I went to lose his secret,
Tried to throw it far away.
But it clung hard to my fingers,
Like ice cubes in a tray.

I've tried to tell my secret
(I'm scared, to tell the truth),
But inside my mouth, the secret
Sticks like toffee to the roof.

By night, it lurks in shadows,
And sneaks into my bed.
Then the secret, like a poltergeist,
Throws tantrums in my head.

Next time he has a secret,
I won't be hanging round.
I'll turn my ghetto blaster up
And drown it in the sound!

Maureen Haselhurst

A Child's Poem

Why is there rain, and where does it come from, Mum?
And how come clouds live up in the sky?
And why did my brother get ill and die?

The rain is a river of tears, my dear,
For every cloud sees how sad we are here.
Yet I don't know why your brother should die.

Why are the leaves so bright and so green, Mum?
And how do they learn to fall off and fly?
And why did my brother get ill and die?

Leaves are alive and filled with breath, my child.
At the end of the year, they have their death.
But I just don't know how my son could die.

And will he ever come back again, Mum?
And can't we find him if we really try?
And I'm so unhappy, Mum, why did he die?

He's taken a boat to the river of tears
And we shall not see him for so many years
So hold my hand, little one, and wave him goodbye.
So hold my hand tight, little one, and wave him goodbye.

Andrew Fusek Peters

Family Portrait

When Mrs Hill says
'Paint your family'
I start all right
With Mum and Dad
And Tom and Kim
And Snowy and Patch,
Then my mind fogs up.

I paint Dad out.
For if he's in
Then so is Samantha
His kind-of wife
And their twins.
But none of them live
At our house.

Keith does.
And at weekends
His kids;
It's a squash.
I paint them taking up
A lot of room.

Then I remember the twins
Are my half-brothers.
So I paint Dad back in
With a very small pram
But not Samantha.

I do blobs to get rid of Keith
And I'm just blobbing his kids
When Mrs Hill says 'Oh dear,
That's a bit of a mess.'

Frances Nagle

Minus One

One from three makes two, they say,
But, since my mother's gone away,
My father's lost his former sense of fun,
And I know that one from three's
A gloomy none.

John Kitching

I Heard Them Shouting

I heard them shouting at each other
Through my bedroom wall
But that was how it often was,
Nothing unusual.

I could never make out their words
Or begin to guess
Exactly what it was this time
Might have started the mess.

Once I lay awake
The whole night through,
Wondering what if anything
I could do.

Were they asleep yet,
Would it start again,
Would it be even louder
Or just the same?

I'd heard them shouting at each other
Through my bedroom wall
And now this silent waiting
Was worst of all.

John Mole

They Still Love Me

Dad doesn't love Mum any more.
He used to once but,
He says they grew apart.
He still loves me though.

Mum doesn't love Dad any more.
She used to once but,
She says he seemed to change.
She still loves me though.

Dad doesn't live here any more.
He used to once but,
He thought it for the best.
He still loves me though.

Mum doesn't cry here any more.
She used to once but,
She gets on with her life.
She still loves me though.

They don't see each other any more.
They used to once but,
They go their separate ways.
They still love me though.

Brenda Williams

Messages

At school
when I'm feeling low
I whisper a secret message into my hand
and hold it tightly in my fist
until playtime.
Then I release my message,
watching it soar
like a carnival balloon
into the speckled sky.

At night,
when Mum has turned out the light,
I think of Dad
and I'm sad that he's dead
but I still have the message
he whispered to me.
I pick up the conch shell
by my bed
and listen again.

I hear him,
like the echo of a shooting star
in the seas of space.
Don't worry, he whispers,
I love you.

Roger Stevens

Ties

Father, mother,
Sister, brother,
Tied one to all,
Each to each other.

Ties that bind
Like solid steel,
Ties you can't see,
Only feel.

Travel far
And then you'll know
Ties that bind
And won't let go.

Father, mother,
Sister, brother,
Tied one to all,
Each to each other.

Tony Bradman

Grandma

I'd like to take a
Plane to Jamaica
With its bright, blue seas
And its great, green palms.

But, most of all
I like to go
And be cuddled and hugged
In my grandma's arms.

John Kitching

Grandad

Grandad's dead
And I'm sorry about that.

He'd a huge black overcoat.
He felt proud in it.
You could have hidden
A football crowd in it.
Far too big—
It was a lousy fit
But Grandad didn't
Mind a bit.
He wore it all winter
With a squashed black hat.

Now he's dead
And I'm sorry about that.

He'd got twelve stories.
I'd heard every one of them
Hundreds of times
But that was the fun of them:
You knew what was coming
So you could join in.
He'd got big hands
And brown, grooved skin
And when he laughed
It knocked you flat.

Now he's dead
And I'm sorry about that.

Kit Wright

Goodbye

My holidays were spent with Gran.
She was very small and very old.
In the evenings she'd tell stories
Of when she was even smaller,
And the saddest one she told
Was about her baby brother
Who they knew was going to die,
So all the family stood in line
To kiss him for the last time
And say goodbye.

She let me do things not allowed at home.
She cooked custard for breakfast
And brought it on a tray to me in bed.
She let me feed the pigeons on the window ledge.
But the best was the day when I said
How I'd like to make a bed in the bath.
So she tied up the taps,
Fetched blankets and sheets,
Lined it with pillows,
And I slept there for the week.

But I outgrew Gran.
As I grew taller she became the child.
My visits grew fewer
And one day when I called
She opened the door and smiled,
'Hello, John. It is John, isn't it?'
'No, Gran. I'm the other one.'
(How could she mistake me for my brother?)

I was too busy growing up for childish games.
Too busy to drop by.

When I had the time,
Her time had run out.
It was too late to say goodbye.

Pat Moon

So you want to be my friend?

Copycats

I like her, I like her not.
We're best of friends, I hate her.
I'm turned to ice or furnace-hot
By my annoying imitator.

We laugh and whisper secrets,
But then she makes me mad,
When everything I choose or buy
She gets! (Or else she's had!)

'You know that dress you bought last week,
You'd been saving for so long?
I told my dad how nice you looked—
Guess what? Now I've got one!'

It's dresses, CDs, songs and crisps,
It's everything that makes *me*.
When I turn to look at her
My reflection's what I see.

Do you know anyone like her?
Does your friend do it too?
If you have found the cure for this,
Please, may I copy you?

Daphne Kitching

Two of a Kind?

I like my friend and he likes me
But he can never come to tea
Mother says he's rude and rough
Talks too loud, acts too tough.
I think he's great, he's really cool
Always breaking every rule.
He knows the answers, wears great gear
Cheeks the teachers, has no fear.
Clowns around, fools about.
Mum says he's just a stupid lout.
She says he's leading me astray
Stops me working every day.
I really don't know what to do
Cos really, I suppose that's true.
But I get bored without him see?
And no one else will sit by me!

Brenda Williams

Why Did You Pull Her Hair?

I told my friend a secret.
She promised not to tell.
My friend told her friend.
Her friend told hers as well.

Now everyone knows my secret.
I think that it's unfair.
I told my friend I trusted her.
That's why I pulled her hair.

John Foster

Betrayal

He told.

I'd wanted to be his friend
And sit next to him at the back.
I'd stuck up for him when things went wrong,
And said *I'd* caused the window to crack.

And he told.

The fun we had when I played the trick,
The pong as the stink bomb fell.
The holding of noses, the coughs and the groans,
The drama of seeming unwell.

And he told her.

Miss Matlock, our teacher, could not see the joke,
She spoke sternly of asthma and danger,
She demanded the name of the culprit,
And then, I saw that my 'friend' was a stranger.

He told her
                it
                        was
                                ME.

He *told* her.

Daphne Kitching

Falling Out

Melanie didn't meet me
Down by the rec at eight.
She wasn't at the corner shop
Or by the school gate.

I couldn't find her on the yard,
She wasn't in the line,
She wasn't there at register
When the clock struck nine.

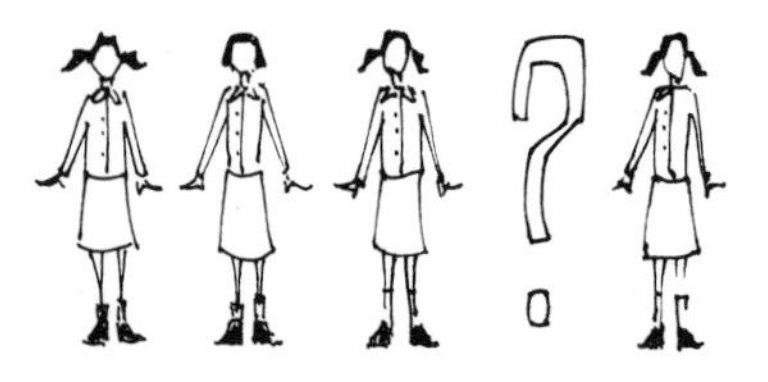

I don't know how it all began
But yesterday we quarrelled.
I said some things I didn't mean;
I really was dead horrid.

The final straw was when she said
She'd go to the park with Dee.
'See if I care!' I'd yelled at her.
'Anne'll be best friends with me!'

But Melanie was my best friend.
I want her for best friend still.
But the way she looked at me yesterday
I don't think she ever will.

I sit at my desk with a lump in my throat
Trying so hard not to cry,
But the words in my reading book sort of swim.
Why did I say those things, *why*?

There's a knock at the door and Ben Mason comes in
With a note from the office for Miss.
As she reads it a frown creases up on her face.
'It's from Melanie's mum,' she says.

Then Miss reads the note out loud in class,
So thank goodness I know it's true.
She isn't away because of me—
Melanie's just got flu!

Patricia Leighton

Round the Bend

my friend
will send me
round the bend

round the bend
and back again

when I visit her
she's never in

when I feel sad
she sits and grins

when I feel glad
she's in a spin

she drives me mad—
I just can't win

but it's not a game
she's my best friend—

the one
who sends me
round the bend

Dave Ward

I Like Emma

I like Emma
but I don't know
if she likes me.
All the boys think
I'm a fool.

I wait outside the school gate
at half-past three
trying to keep my cool.
Emma walks past,
shaking her blonde hair free,
laughs with her friends
and drifts off home for tea.

Emma's two years
older than me.
Her class is higher
up the school.

I like Emma
but I don't know
if she likes me.
All the boys
think I'm a fool.

Wes Magee

Junior Disco

Hall curtains drawn
Strobe lights flashing
DJ's first number
Sir on the door.
Floor nearly empty
But groups in the corners
Whispering, giggling
Watching.

Stomach turns over
Throat's in a knot
Ears are tingling.
Do I look all right?
I feel like a freak
But it's too late now—
The gang behind's pushing me—in we go!

Floor's filling up
And the music's good
Everyone's stamping
Clapping, chanting
My cheeks are hot
I'm feeling puffed
But it's great—fantastic!
Never want it to stop!

Time to change tracks
The room stops spinning.
Who's that grinning
And coming this way?
Andy Lee—and I think
—I think—he's going to
Ask me to dance!

I'll say 'Yeh'—cool, like.

Patricia Leighton

Freak

Why do I start walking
half in the gutter, half on the kerb,
or wave my arms like a lunatic,
why does everything I say sound absurd?

My voice is always AWOL
whenever I start to speak,
the words in my mouth are like boulders,
she must think I'm some sort of freak.

Why is it when I take her hand
mine's all clammy and cold?
She's always calm and confident,
I feel about three years old.

Mum says it's just a phase
and my gawkiness will pass,
but I really do like her a lot,
more than anyone else in our class.

And thinking about it I can't believe
I've any chance of success
when I ask if I can see her again
but she looks at me and says, 'Yes!'

Brian Moses

There's Something About Jennifer Timmins

There's something about Jennifer Timmins
Which doesn't seem quite right
And it's got me thinking about her
All day and all through the night.

She hasn't changed much, to tell the truth
She looks exactly the same,
So why do I get so excited
At the mention of her name?

Why does my heart begin to beat,
Why does it go bangabangaboom,
When Jennifer Sarah Timmins
Walks into the classroom?

How come I don't know what to say
When she speaks to me?
How come it's just her face
I'm always glad to see?

Her eyes are still the same shade of blue
And her hair just as blonde as before,
So why do I want to be near her
More and more and more?

Yeah, there's something about Jennifer Timmins
Which doesn't seem quite right,
And it's made me look at her
In a completely different light.

Tony Langham

Friends

I fear it's very wrong of me
And yet I must admit
When someone offers friendship
I want the *whole* of it.
I don't want everybody else
To share my friends with me.
At least, I want *one* special one,
Who, indisputably
  Likes me much more than all the rest,
Who's always on my side.
Who never cares what others say,
Who lets me come and hide
Within his shadow, in his house—
It doesn't matter where—
Who let's me simply be myself,
Who's always, *always* there.

Elizabeth Jennings

Jeers and Tears

Shame

There's a girl at school
we teased today;
made jokes, called her names.
My friends all laughed,
called it harmless fun,
said it was just a game.

Now I'm at home
feeling horrid inside,
long gone that thoughtless grin.
How will I face her
tomorrow at school?
I wish I hadn't joined in.

Tracey Blance

Like a boomerang, mean w
your friend's back can come back to you.

Haiku

Like a boomerang,
mean words behind your friend's back
can come back to you.

Mike Jubb

'Big Boys' Don't Cry

'Big boys' do cry—
When nobody's looking
Or the teacher's back is turned;
In the corner of the park,
When they get home,
(Under the duvet cover).

'Big boys' do cry
Because words that sting
Can be flung so hard
That they can target
A 'big boy's' heart,
And stab out the tears.

Coral Rumble

Names

They call you names for the fun of it,
To make your insides weak,
To injure all of your happiness
And tell you you're a SIKH.

To them you're totally different,
To them you're Lower Class,
They'll hit you and hurt you as much as they can
Till your insides are eaten at last.

They say that you're brown and they hate you,
And they never ever go away,
They've become a part of your life now,
And I fear that they're here to stay.

Kiran Chahal

The Traveller's Child

Shrug your shoulders, Carrie-Claire,
Shrug to show that you don't care,
When they say you're gypsy wild,
A hippy's kid, a traveller's child.
They say you're different from us,
Your home's a double-decker bus.
They say you're odd to want to stay
In that lay-by near the motorway,
Parked up where dirt and rubbish blow.
Perhaps you've nowhere else to go.

Shrug your shoulders, Carrie-Claire,
Shrug when nosy people stare.
You don't fit in, you don't belong,
They sigh relief when you move on.
But when summer trees fly leaves like kites,
You're up and off, you fly-by-nights.
You'll camp high on a wild flower hill
And for a while you'll stay, until
You journey back from summer days
To winter and the motorway.

Maureen Haselhurst

The Diary of a Brace

Week 1
My mouth is a prison with a portcullis gate. Metal muzzled—a razor blade bit. Words ooze through the bars all ugly and lisped. I'll never get used to it!

Week 2
They're calling me Shredder, or Grinder, or worse. Can't handle the hurt and the rage. Try hard to be witty to show I don't care, but my jokes can't escape from their cage.

Week 3
Caught sight of my man-trap reflection today. See why I'm called Cow-Catcher Lips. I suddenly smiled and I laughed at myself and discovered I grin like a zip!

Week 4
When I call myself Tin Grin, they leave me alone. My brace will come off in a while. I'm not really mean, but part of me hopes they'll envy my film star smile!

Maureen Haselhurst

As the Saying Goes . . .

'Sticks and stones
may break my bones
but words will never hurt me . . .'

like pig-face; smelly;
nerd-brain; slag;
like ugly witch
or bag or hag . . .

Sticks and stones
may miss my bones
and breaks, in time, will heal;
but words remain
as does the pain
their memory makes me feel:

. . . the saying never goes.

Celia Warren

Me

I come to school
in the back of a taxi,
for my hands are twisted and torn.

I cannot see well
and my legs are quite weak,
for this was the way I was born.

So, if you see me
sat still in my chair,
please don't just look away.

For I'm really alive
I'm ready to learn,
from each and every new day.

Andrew Collett

Shylock

'If you prick me, do I not bleed.'

If I feel it
perhaps others feel it too.
I don't like being hit
and nor do you.

What Shylock said
is true
both for the Christian
and the Jew.

If we would want
to know how others feel
ask yourself
what things appeal
and what do not.

David Scott

Skulking in Shadows

I Told a Lie Today

I told a lie today
and it curled up inside me
like a steel hard spring.

It was quite a clever lie,
no one guessed the truth,
they believed me.

But I've carried the twist of it
at the centre of my body, all day,
and I think it's expanding,
filling me up,
making my eyes feel red.

Perhaps it's going to uncoil suddenly
and burst me open,
showing everyone what I'm really like.

I think I had better confess,
before I'm completely unwound.

Robin Mellor

The Purse

I pinched it from my mother's purse,
Pretending it's a game.
My muscles tightened: hard and tense.
I pinched it just the same.

'I need it as a loan,' I said.
'It's not against the law.'
'I won't do it again,' I said.
I've said all that before.

The reason was the cash at first,
It isn't any more;
I do it . . . well . . . because I do,
I don't know what it's for.

I only know that when the house
Is silent, empty, still,
I head towards my parents' room
As if against my will.

The sweat is cold upon my neck,
My back and arms feel strange,
I'm sure that someone's watching me
As I pick out her change.

But no one ever catches me,
Sometimes I wish they would;
Then perhaps I'd stop and think
And give it up for good.

But my mum trusts me, buys me things:
Each kindness makes it worse
Because I know, when she's next door
My hands will find her purse.

David Kitchen

Trouble?

Has someone told? And if so, who?
I sit on the hard bench outside
the Head's room, and I'm in a stew.
See me now, the message said.
Time's dragging. I wish I was dead.
Has someone told? And if so, who?

Am I in trouble, or what, *what*?
The long corridor lies empty,
then a door slams like a pistol shot.
Someone shouts. Faint cheers from the Hall.
I stare at the pictures on the wall.
Am I in trouble, or what, *what*?

Who's been telling tales, and why, *why*?
Muffled voices from the Head's room.
Mother told me: tell the truth, never lie.
In her office the Secretary starts to sing.
I hear the telephone ring and ring.
Who's been telling tales, and why, *why*?

What will happen? *Has* someone told?
I fidget. Soon there is the chink
of cups and saucers. I feel cold.
Up the corridor comes Andrea Line,
sees me and gives the thumbs-down sign.
What will happen? *Has* someone told?

What's it about? Won't someone say?
I've been here . . . hours. It's almost break.
My friends will soon go out to play.
I've been forgotten. I feel ill.
I'm in a state and I can't sit still.
What's it about? Oh, won't someone say?

Wes Magee

Things That I Shouldn't Have Done

Things that I do that I shouldn't
are things that I shouldn't have done,
and the things that I haven't but I ought to
are the things that I ought to have done.
But things that I shouldn't and oughtn't
are things I wouldn't have done
if the should and the would had been easier
and the should not had not been such fun.

David Scott

Sorry

Why is the word 'sorry'
So very hard to say?
Your mouth goes dry,
Your arms go stiff,
Your knees start to give way.
And even when that little word
Is ready to pop out,
It rolls around
Upon your tongue
Until you have to shout,
'I'M SORRY!', just to get it past
Your gums, your teeth, your lips;
And then your mum says,
'Well, my girl,
'It doesn't sound like it!'

Coral Rumble

Jealousy

Jealousy is like a great black
hole sucking everything
in.
Jealousy is like a fungus
growing and growing inside.
Like a monster punching me inside.
Like a star burning up.
Like a bee-sting right inside
that's
what
jealousy is.

Terry Baylis (age 8)

Hate

Hate is like a cancer
It starts small
But grows
And gradually affects all.
Sometimes it spreads slowly
Unnoticed at first
But then
Infects everyone.
It taints and spoils.
Hate kills love
and poisons minds.
It swarms through crowds
and fuels riots.
Hate destroys
And causes wars.

Brenda Williams

Who Cares?

Too Much

I turn the TV off:
I cannot bear to look.
I cannot bear to hear the hungry cough;
To see the flies round haunted eyes;
To see the bulging belly
Or the needle bone.
I hide myself alone
And bury eyes and ears and mind,
And try so hard to find
Escape or brighter shape
Inside the words of this slight book.

I turn the TV off:
I cannot bear to look.

John Kitching

Just Another War

On her sideboard
Nan has a picture
Of a young man
In a soldier's uniform
Smiling proudly.

'That's my brother,
Your Uncle Reg,'
She says,
Her voice tinged
With sadness.

'He was killed
In Korea.
He was only nineteen.'

'Where's Korea?' I say.
'What were they fighting for?'

'Somewhere in Asia,'
She says.
'I don't know.
It was just another war.'

John Foster

Rainbow of Suffering

Red is in the eyes of a mother
  mourning her child.
Orange is in parched fields
  burning under the sun.
Yellow is in careless coins
  scattered at a beggar's feet.
Green is in shallow wells
  drying in the drought.
Blue is in the ungloved hands
  of a Bosnian boy in winter.
Indigo is in swollen bruises
  on a battered child's face.
Violet is in the loneliness
  of an old woman's memories.
Suffering is in a coloured bridge
  across a wounded world.

Moira Andrew

Dunblane

13 March 1996

Dear Lord, help me.
The Minister says that I shall
hear my friends' voices in the wind of morning.
That their small hands will touch my own with the evening breeze.
He says that their tears shall fall as gentle rain on my face,
and their gift of laughter warm me with the sun.
The Minister says that my friends
will walk with me in the wakeful light of dawn,
and that the sound of their names will be a song forever
for sparrows in the playground,
(whatever *that* means).
But, Lord, why can't they play Hopscotch with me
On Thursdays?

Lucy Coats

Just One Day

Mum lost her job and couldn't pay
the rent
so they took our home away.

From a flat
                        to the street
took just one day.
Now people rush past
and look away
they think only animals
live this way.

So spare some change or just some time—
Homelessness is not a crime.
I'm a person—my name is Caroline.

Lindsay Macrae

Coming Late

Isabel comes late to school.
Tight as a bud in winter
into herself she curls
when our teacher reprimands her.

You are a slack and lazy girl.
You won't be any good . . .
(The voice has risen to a howl
of wind above a frozen wood)

. . . until you learn to come on time
and take more pride and show you care.
Isabel hides a living pain
beneath her blank and frosted stare.

She cannot say her dad has gone,
her mum is ill, she has to dress
and feed her brothers, copes alone
without complaint; will not confess

her courage in a shrivelled life,
will not admit to anyone
that deep inside her is a fragile leaf
craving some warmth to open in the sun.

Barrie Wade

Touching

This is a song
about touch and touching.
You touch me—a way of feeling.
I touch you—a way of understanding.
We are touched
by a film or a book.
We are touched
when a stranger is kind.
How can we live
without touching and being touched?

There is a healing touch,
it makes the sick whole again.
Let's keep in touch
we say to a friend who's going away.
To have the right touch
means to know how it's done.
Touching is an art,
it's the movement
to and from the heart.

Some are easily touched.
Some are hard to touch.
You are often touched.
I am often touched.

Nissim Ezekiel

On the outside, looking in

The Lonely Place

On the outside, looking in,
she watched the others.
She watched the bustling,
and the hustling
and the way they herded
together like sheep.
They liked the same things.
The same old soaps on TV.
The same old people.
Same old games.
She was different.
Even so.
Sometimes,
watching them
shouting and laughing
she wished
that being on the outside, looking in,
was not such a lonely place.

Marian Swinger

Left Out

It feels as if pins
Are pricking my eyes.
My face is burning hot.
A firework is trying
To go off inside me.
My feet are glued to the spot.
My hands are rocks in my pockets.
I want to run away,
But my legs are rooted to the ground
Like trees. I have to stay
And listen
To everyone calling me names
And not letting me
Join in with their games.

Celia Warren

Who?

I am the child that you never hear,
whose face you don't see.
I work with my head down, silently.

I am the child who is always alone,
whose name you don't know.
Deserts flake in my eyes like snow.

I sit at the back—
my voice on a thread in my eyes,
walled by glass—
        I'm foreign, I'm strange,
        I'm new in your class.

Jane Thorp

Heavy Load

I wish I could pick up my feelings and put them in a sack
I'd sling it over my shoulders and carry them on my back
I'd take them to the river and watch them float away
Maybe after doing that I'd start to feel OK.

Tammy Lynn

The Sun Will Shine

'Don't be glum,' says Mum.
'Don't be sad,' says Dad.
'The coal-black sack of gloom
Inside your roomy head
Will go, we know,' they say.
'Your sadness is not here to stay.
We see your ears and eyes today
Are full of sights and sounds of sorrow.
But, believe us, dear, we do know
The sun will rise.
There will be sun again
Some fine tomorrow.'

John Kitching

Give Yourself A Hug

Give yourself a hug
when you feel unloved

Give yourself a hug
when people put on airs
to make you feel a bug

Give yourself a hug
when everyone seems to give you
a cold-shoulder shrug

Give yourself a hug—
a big big hug

And keep on singing,
'Only one in a million like me
Only one in a million-billion-trillion-zillion
like me.'

Grace Nichols

Looking to the Future

Yesterday

Yesterday I knew all the answers
Or I knew my parents did.

Yesterday I had my Best Friend
And my Second Best Friend
And I knew whose Best Friend I was
And who disliked me.

Yesterday I hated asparagus and coconut and parsnips
And mustard and pickles and olives
And anything I'd never tasted.

Yesterday I knew what was Right and what was Wrong
And I never had any trouble deciding which was which.
It always seemed so obvious.

But today . . . everything's changing.
I suddenly have a million unanswered questions.
Everybody I meet might become a friend.
I tried eating snails with garlic sauce—and I liked them!
And I know the delicate shadings that lie between
Good and evil—and I face their dilemma.
Life is harder now . . . and yet, easier . . .
And more and more exciting!

Jean Little

Index of Titles and First Lines

(First lines are in italics)

Index of Authors

Inside artwork by

Stan Chow

Warwick Johnson Cadwell

Turinna Gren

Acknowledgements

We would like to thank the following for permission to include their poems, published here for the first time:
Moira Andrew: 'The Sun in Me' and 'Rainbow of Suffering', both copyright © Moira Andrew 2000; Ann Bonner: 'Cheer Up', copyright © Ann Bonner 2000; Tony Bradman: 'Ties', copyright © Tony Bradman 2000; Debjani Chatterjee: 'Acrostic', copyright © Debjani Chatterjee 2000; Lucy Coats: 'Dunblane, 13 March 1996', copyright © Lucy Coats 2000; Andrew Collett: 'Me', copyright © Andrew Collett 2000; Maureen Haselhurst: 'The Secret', 'The Traveller's Child', and 'The Story of a Brace', all copyright © Maureen Haselhurst 2000; David Kitchen: 'The Purse', copyright © David Kitchen 2000; Daphne Kitching: 'Copycats', and 'Betrayal', both copyright © Daphne Kitching 2000; John Kitching: 'Too Much', 'Minus One', 'Grandma', and 'The Sun Will Shine', all copyright © John Kitching 2000; Tony Langham: 'There's Something About Jennifer Timmins', copyright © Tony Langham 2000; Patricia Leighton: 'Junior Disco', 'A Head Full of Feelings', and 'Falling Out', all copyright © Patricia Leighton 2000; Wes Magee: 'I Like Emma', copyright © Wes Magee 2000; Brian Moses: 'Day', copyright © Brian Moses 2000; Frances Nagle: 'Sisterly Love' and 'Family Portrait', both copyright © Frances Nagle 2000; Judith Nicholls: 'Mountain', copyright © Judith Nicholls 2000; John Rice: 'Big Fears', copyright © John Rice 2000; Fred Sedgwick: 'Kelly Jane Alone', copyright © Fred Sedgwick 2000; Roger Stevens: 'Messages', copyright © Roger Stevens 2000; Marian Swinger: 'The Lonely Place', 'Why Me?', and 'Night Fears', all copyright © Marian Swinger 2000; Jane Thorp: 'Who?', copyright © Jane Thorp 2000; Dave Ward: 'Round the Bend', copyright © Dave Ward 2000; Celia Warren: 'As the Saying Goes . . .', copyright © Celia Warren 2000; Brenda Williams: 'They Still Love Me', 'Two of a Kind', and 'Hate' all copyright © Brenda Williams 2000.

We are also grateful for permission to include the following poems:
David Bateson: 'Special Day', first published in *A Puddin' Rich and Rare*, New South Wales School Magazine Anthology (NSW Department of Education, 1988), reprinted by permission of Mrs E. Bateson; Terry Baylis: 'Jealousy' from Jennifer Curry (ed.): *Wondercrump 3* (Red Fox), reprinted by permission of the Random House Group Ltd; Tracey Blance: 'Shame', copyright © Tracey Blance 1999, first published in Tony Bradman (ed.): *I Wanna Be Your Mate* (Bloomsbury, 1999), reprinted by permission of the author; Kiran Chahal: 'Names', copyright © Kiran Chahal 1985, first published in Adrian Mitchell (ed.): *Strawberry Drums* (Macdonald Young Books, 1985), reprinted by permission of the author; Sharon Cheeks: 'S-t-r-e-t-c-h-i-n-g' from *Cadbury's Second Selection of Children's Poetry*, reprinted by permission of Cadbury Ltd; Wendy Cope: 'Huff', copyright © Wendy Cope 1987, and 'The Baby of the Family', copyright © Wendy Cope 1991, reprinted by permission of the author; Berlie Doherty: 'First Leap' from *Walking on Air* (HarperCollins), reprinted by permission of David Higham Associates; Gina Douthwaite: 'How Do I Feel?' from *Myself* (Scholastic, 1996), copyright © Gina Douthwaite 1996, reprinted by permission of the author; Nissim Ezekiel: 'Touching' from *Latter-Day Psalms*, (OUP, India), reprinted by permission of the publisher; John Foster: 'Why Did You Pull Her Hair?', copyright © John Foster 1995 from John Foster (ed.): *Feelings Poems* (OUP, 1995), and 'Just Another War' from *Five O'Clock Friday* (OUP, 1991), copyright © John Foster 1991, reprinted by permission of the author; Elizabeth Jennings: 'Friends' from *The Secret Brother* (Macmillan), reprinted by permission of David Higham Associates; Mike Jubb: 'Haiku' ('Like a boomerang'), copyright © Mike Jubb 1999, first published in *I Wanna Be Your Mate* (Bloomsbury, 1999), reprinted by permission of the author; Jean Little: 'Yesterday I Knew All the Answers' from *Hey World, Here I Am*, copyright © 1986 Jean Little, reprinted by permission of Kids Can Press Ltd, Toronto and HarperCollins Publishers Inc.; Tammy Lynn: 'Heavy Load' first published in *The Times Educational Supplement*, 17 April 1998 reprinted by permission of the Head of Walworth School, London, on behalf of the author; Lindsay Macrae: 'Just One Day' from *You Canna Shove Yer Granny Off a Bus* (Viking, 1995), copyright © Lindsay Macrae 1995, reprinted by permission of Penguin Books Ltd and of The Agency (London) Ltd. All rights reserved and enquiries to The Agency (London) Ltd.; Roger McGough: 'Scowling' from *Pillow Talk* (Viking), copyright © Roger McGough, reprinted by permission of The Peters Fraser & Dunlop Group Ltd on behalf of the author; Wes Magee: 'Trouble' from *Morning Break, and Other Poems* (Cambridge University Press, 1989), copyright © Wes Magee 1989, reprinted by permission of the author; Robin Mellor: 'I Told a Lie Today', copyright © Robin Mellor 1994, first published in *Assemblies* (Scholastic, 1994); John Mole: 'Everybody' from *The Conjuror's Rabbit* (Blackie, 1992), copyright © John Mole 1992, and 'I Heard them Shouting' from *The Dummy's Dilemma* (Hodder, 1999), copyright © John Mole 1999, both reprinted by permission of the author; Pat Moon: 'Goodbye' from *Earthlings* (Pimlico, 1991) copyright © Pat Moon 1991, reprinted by permission of the author; Brian Moses: 'Freak', copyright © Brian Moses 1991, first published in Tony Bradman (ed.): *Our Side of the Playground* (Bodley Head, 1991), reprinted by permission of the author; Grace Nichols: 'Give Yourself a Hug' from *Give Yourself a Hug* (A. & C. Black, 1994), © Grace Nichols 1994, reprinted by permission of Curtis Brown Ltd., London; Andrew Fusek Peters: 'A Child's Poem', copyright © Andrew Fusek Peters 1991, first published in *May the Angels Be With Us* (Shropshire Education Publications, 1994), reprinted by permission of the author; Jack Prelutsky: 'I'm in a Rotten Mood' from *The New Kid on the Block*, copyright © Jack Prelutsky 1984, reprinted by permission of the publishers, Heinemann Young Books, an imprint of Egmont Children's Books Ltd, London; Coral Rumble: 'Big Boys Don't Cry' from *Creatures, Teachers and Family Features* (Macdonald Young Books, 1999), copyright © Coral Rumble 1999, and 'Sorry', copyright © Coral Rumble 1997, first published in Pat Alexander (ed.): *A Feast of Good Stories* (Lion, 1997), both reprinted by permission of the author; David Scott: 'Shylock' and 'Things that I Shouldn't Have Done' from *How Does it Feel* (Blackie); Barrie Wade: 'Coming Late' from *Barley, Barley* (OUP), reprinted by permission of the author; Celia Warren: 'Left Out' first published in John Foster (ed.): *Feelings Poems* (OUP, 1995) copyright © Celia Warren 1995, reprinted by permission of the author; John Whitworth: 'Boring' from *Casting a Spell* compiled by Angela Heth (Orchard), reprinted by permission of the author; Abigail Wright: 'I Hate Being Dyslexic', copyright © Abigail Wright 1989, first published in W.H. Smiths' *Young Words* (Macmillan Children's Books, 1989), reprinted by permission of the author; Kit Wright: 'Grandad' from *Rebating On* (HarperCollins, 1978), reprinted by permission of the author.

Despite every effort to trace and contact copyright holders before publication this has not been possible in all cases. If notified the publisher will be pleased to rectify any errors or omissions at the earliest opportunity.